T0349803

THE LITTLE BOOK OF
MAGICK

ASTRID CARVEL

summersdale

THE LITTLE BOOK OF MAGICK

Copyright © Octopus Publishing Group Limited, 2024

All rights reserved.

Text by Susan McCann

No part of this book may be reproduced by any means, nor transmitted, nor translated into a machine language, without the written permission of the publishers.

Condition of Sale
This book is sold subject to the condition that it shall not, by way of trade or otherwise, be lent, resold, hired out or otherwise circulated in any form of binding or cover other than that in which it is published and without a similar condition including this condition being imposed on the subsequent purchaser.

An Hachette UK Company
www.hachette.co.uk

Summersdale Publishers
Part of Octopus Publishing Group Limited
Carmelite House
50 Victoria Embankment
LONDON
EC4Y 0DZ
UK

www.summersdale.com

Printed and bound in Poland

ISBN: 978-1-83799-413-7

This FSC® label means
that materials used for
the product have been
responsibly sourced

MIX
Paper | Supporting
responsible forestry
FSC® C018236

Substantial discounts on bulk quantities of Summersdale books are available to corporations, professional associations and other organizations. For details contact general enquiries: telephone: +44 (0) 1243 771107 or email: enquiries@summersdale.com.

CONTENTS

✦ INTRODUCTION ✦

Welcome to the wonderful world of magick!

A fascination with the supernatural may have led you here... you may have been itching to discover how working with the magickal forces of the universe can be both life-enhancing and enormous fun!

Mystical and mysterious, illuminating and powerful, the practice of magick offers you the opportunity to grab life by the scruff of the neck and influence your own destiny.

By learning how to work in harmony with nature and about fascinating otherworldly deities, magickal symbols, rituals, spells and tools, we can make the world a happier place.

This book will cover all of those things and more, giving you the basics to become a modern witch.

You should bear in mind the threefold law, or Wiccan rede, used by many magicians: what you put out there comes back to you threefold. So always remember to use your magick as a force for good.

The power for change is at your fingertips!

WHAT IS MAGICK?

We're all familiar with the word magic, so let's answer the question on the tip of our tongues...

What's the difference between magic and magick?

Magic refers to the practice of illusion often performed onstage by magicians.

Magick encompasses a variety of beliefs, traditions and practices and is the ritualization of spiritual intentions that bring about real-life changes. It includes the use of meditation, spells, symbols and other tools and is commonly linked with the occult, meaning the study of hidden knowledge (derived from the Latin *occultus*, "hidden" or "secret").

The Pluralism Project, which studies religious diversity in the United States, defines this alternate spelling as separating "the spiritual practice from the fictional magic of fantasy novels and films".

Although "magic" and "magick" are often used interchangeably, there is a key difference in intention.

Magick is seen as a tool for spiritual growth, while magic is a form of entertainment.

This chapter will look at magickal groups and beliefs, along with magickal tools, deities, symbols and the importance of nature.

✦ MAGICK WITH A "K" ✦

Magick was first officially spelled with a "k" by British occultist Aleister Crowley (1875-1947), who wanted his spiritual practice to be recognized as different from stage magic.

Crowley defined magick as any action that moves a person towards fulfilling their ultimate destiny, or "one's true will". On this basis, he founded a religion named Thelema, from the Greek *thelēma,* meaning "will".

Crowley had other reasons for spelling "magick" the way he did. The numbers six and eleven were significant to him, so it's no coincidence he extended the word "magic" to the six letters of "magick", and that "k" is the eleventh letter of the alphabet. (See pages 114-115 for more about numerology.)

A controversial figure, Crowley died in obscurity and had few followers during his lifetime. However, he became a cult figure after his death and influenced other modern religious founders such as Wicca's Gerald Gardner. He even features on the album cover of *Sgt. Pepper's Lonely Hearts Club Band* by The Beatles.

MAGICKAL GROUPS AND FOLLOWERS

Magick can be practised as a group or alone. There's a variety of practitioners across the globe, but the main magickal groups in this book include:

- **Hermetic Qabalah** – movement based on Jewish mysticism, Hellenic (Classical Greek) magick and Hermeticism (a branch of ancient spiritual philosophy).
- **Witchcraft** – a practice as old as time itself. Witches practise alone or in a collective called a coven.
- **Wicca** – said to be the foundation of modern witchcraft.
- **Thelema** – created by Aleister Crowley, Thelemites are influenced by Hermetic Qabalah and the Hermetic Order of the Golden Dawn (see page 53).
- **Goddess movement** – movement that seeks to correct the balance of patriarchal-heavy religion by connecting to the divine feminine and promoting goddess worship.
- **Shamanism** – deriving from Africa, shamans often carry out work to heal the sick by entering a trance state.
- **Vodou** – misunderstood monotheistic religion from Africa, influenced by displaced slaves.
- **Druidry and neo-druidism** – ancient and modern religion particularly linked to nature and the landscape.

✦ WHO PRACTISES MAGICK? ✦

Someone who practises magick is often referred to as a magician, sorcerer, witch or shaman. They can play a central role in some societies, while they may find themselves ostracized in others.

The term magician is sometimes confused with the word conjuror, reflecting some historical confusion. In this book, the term magician refers to one who practises magick, rather than one who practises magic and stage illusion.

"Magician" derives from the word for an ancient Persian priest (*magus*), and *maghdim*, a Chaldean term meaning wisdom and philosophy (Chaldea was a Babylonian nation in modern southern Iraq). In European history, the power of magicians to summon evil has often been feared, but magick can be neutral. In many societies, a magician can protect others from harm or help with spiritual growth.

✦ MAGICKAL PRACTICES ✦

Magicians throughout the world carry out a wide variety of practices that vary with culture and tradition. They range from spell-casting to reading cat behaviour!

Ritualization is the key component to a magickal practice, meaning that the magician partakes in a sequence of symbolic and repetitive actions to obtain a particular result. Some groups, such as witches, create a circle for protection, while others work with a pentacle (Wiccans) or pentagram (various neopagan groups). Once you've cleansed and created your protective space, you can use a variety of the tools covered in this chapter (and perhaps some that aren't!) to cast a spell or carry out other ritualistic magick that involves manifesting your intentions into reality.

Divination, the ancient art of gaining insight into a situation (see pages 80–83), is also important in magick. The Romans used to read animal entrails, but, today, we think of divination more as involving tarot cards or crystal balls, although runes and their Chinese equivalent, the *I Ching*, are still popular.

Magickal practices are covered in detail in the Practising Magick chapter, from page 93.

✦.✲ MAGICKAL BELIEFS ✲•✦

The magician's belief falls outside the major world religions, such as Christianity, Judaism, Islam, Hinduism and Buddhism. Many magicians therefore identify with some system of paganism, an umbrella term that describes a diverse group of religious and spiritual belief systems.

Most pagan-inspired religions:

- Are polytheist (meaning they believe in more than one deity), animist (all things have a spirit), or pantheist (the divine is in everything)

- Revere nature and its seasonal cycles

- Are based on ancient, pre-Christian belief systems such as witchcraft, Hellenism or Norse traditions

The word "pagan" originates from the Latin *paganus*, once meaning "rustic" and later meaning "civilian". Paganism was originally a derogatory term used towards the end of the Roman Empire, and Christians used it to identify non-Christians who worshipped numerous gods and goddesses. Only in modern times have pagans used this word to describe themselves or their religious practices. Modern paganism is sometimes referred to as neopaganism, although many practitioners still use the term paganism.

✦.✦ MAGICKAL DEITIES ✦•✦

A deity is a god or goddess who can assist you in your magickal practice by providing guidance, protection and specific energies. Magickal practitioners are often drawn towards working with gods and goddesses from pre-Christian times and associate specific deities with certain rituals.

There are so many ancient gods and goddesses that it's impossible to list them all! But rest assured that there's one for every conceivable thing: deities of the sky and stars, birth and death, love and war, the home and even poetry!

Here are a few well-known magickal deities from around the world:

Area of expertise	God/Goddess	Belief system
Magick	Hecate, the mother of Witchcraft	Greek
Love	Cupid, Venus	Roman
Wisdom	Odin	Norse
Healing, fertility, wisdom, water	Anahit	Armenian
Transformation, meditation	Shiva	Hindu
Water, motherhood, fertility	Yemaya	African

✦ MAGICKAL TOOLS ✦

In the following pages, we'll look at some of the magickal tools you can use as a magician. Here's a summary of the ones you could use:

- **Wand** – a special stick for directing magickal power
- **Crystal ball** – gaze into a crystal ball to see into your future
- **Cauldron** – the witch's legendary stewing pot, brewing anything from lunch to spells
- **Broom** – legendary common household implement, associated particularly with witches
- **Grimoire** – a book of magickal spells
- **Altar** – somewhere solid to display all your tools
- **Candles** – these enhance the magickal ambience, and you can also engrave them with words or symbols to add potency to spells
- **Crystals** – these delightful gems channel nature's power as well as supernatural powers
- **Herbs** – the little green plants you use in everyday cooking are more powerful than you know!
- **Chalice** – an elegant goblet or cup used to drink from in rituals
- **Athame** – a dull (blunt) ceremonial blade that's used only for ritualistic purposes
- **Pendulum** – a weighted object hung from a chain or cord, used for divination and dowsing

✦ WAND ✦

A wand is an essential tool for any budding magician! Wands are used to direct magickal energy and amplify an intention during spell-casting rituals.

They're usually made from natural materials, such as wood or metal, and you may want to think about the properties each adds to your spell when choosing one. Wands themselves are associated with masculine energy.

You can buy wands online, in a local esoteric shop, or have a go at making one yourself. Enhance your chances of success by using one of the following wands:

- **Oak** – brings luck and longevity as you work your magick
- **Birch, pine, alder** – protective, cleansing, grounding
- **Beech** – attracts love, friendship and job opportunities
- **Maple** – enhances spells relating to prosperity and abundance
- **Gold** – enhances beauty, attracts love and abundance
- **Silver** – amplifies psychic abilities, good for moon magick
- **Tin** – divination spells, attracts good luck
- **Copper** – brings love and abundance
- **Brass** – encourages communication, good for protective spells
- **Steel** – promotes healing and protection
- **Zinc** – banishment and protection spells, attracts love and prosperity

✦.✳ CRYSTAL BALL ✴˚✦

These wonderful magickal objects have been used in many cultures and date back to at least the first century CE, when Pliny the Elder wrote about soothsayers gazing into a crystal ball.

John Dee, consultant to Queen Elizabeth I of England in the late sixteenth century, consulted a crystal ball and their popularity later soared during the Victorian era.

Widely used in the Middle Ages, travellers and Romani people carried the tradition from India to Europe, and they continue to fascinate today, used mostly by psychics and mediums.

They're often made from glass or clear quartz crystal and can come in a variety of different sizes. They can be used for the following magickal purposes:

- **Scrying** – gaze into the ball to "see" messages from the universe (see pages 102–103)
- **Meditation** – hold the ball or have it near you during meditation to deepen your practice
- **Healing** – place the ball over any blocked chakras

The Dowager Empress Crystal Ball, weighing 22 kg (49 lb), is one of the largest crystal balls in the world and is thought to have belonged to the Qing dynasty of China.

✦ CAULDRON ✦

These pots, traditionally made of iron, are a well-known magickal tool of witches everywhere.

While historically they may have been used for cooking, cleaning or carrying water, in European witch lore they became famous for the brewing of poisons and ointments or for ritualistic use in spell-casting. The continuous stirring of the cauldron was thought by Celts to combine divine wisdom and inspiration with the cycle of life, death and rebirth. Considered a feminine symbol, the cauldron also symbolizes the womb of the mother goddess.

In medieval art, literature and folklore, the cauldron could be seen bubbling over a roaring fire in the house of every witch. During the witch hunts of the late sixteenth and seventeenth centuries, witches were accused of creating spells using ingredients such as bats' blood, snakes, decapitated toads and baby fat.

However, cauldrons were essential to alchemists looking to change lead into gold or silver, or to create a large gem from small ones.

Famous cauldrons

The Cauldron of Regeneration is associated with the Celtic goddesses Cerridwen and Branwen, along with the Babylonian goddess Siris. Their cauldrons also provided wisdom and inspiration.

The Gundestrup Cauldron from Denmark, dated 100 BCE and made of silver, is engraved with images of unlucky victims being thrown into a sacrificial cauldron. Sacrificial cauldrons also appear in shamanic and Celtic traditions.

The Cauldron of Dyrnwch, the ancient Welsh god, is said to separate a brave man from a coward. The braver the man, the quicker the meat would cook. If you were cooking dinner for a coward, you might still be waiting for it now, as the meat would never cook!

The Norse god Odin drank magic blood from a cauldron of wisdom to obtain divine power, while the Greek witch goddess, Medea, could restore youth to those lucky enough to drink from her cauldron!

✦ ·✦ BROOM ✦ᐟᵒ✦

Most known for their association with witchcraft, the broom or besom is a traditional magickal tool often used to sweep a ceremonial area to cleanse it before a ritual. As well as helpfully cleaning the floor (!) it symbolically clears any negative energies that have built up since the last ritual.

Brooms are easy to make and were an established part of ancient ritualistic practices. In many cultures, they were thought to have magickal properties, believed to protect homes, consecrate sacred spaces, and assist in divination and spirit communication. Hand-sized versions have even been discovered in tombs in ancient Egypt, thought to have been placed there to sweep away negative energy.

Traditionally, a besom (from the Old English *besma*) is made of birch twigs, with a staff of ash or oak, bound by strips of willow or hazel. The besom is now becoming popular as a feature of pagan or Wiccan wedding ceremonies, where the happy couple "jump the broom" to enter their new life together and affirm their commitment.

Your magickal broom can be used for many different tasks other than sweeping, and you might have several for varying purposes.

- Adorn a broom with green ribbons and work with it in prosperity rituals. You could also embed some crystals that vibe with prosperity and good fortune, such as aventurine, into the handle, or carve the appropriate symbols of abundance-attracting runes.

- Hang a broom above your front door to keep undesirable guests and negative energy away. This is also said to deflect curses and nasty gossip.

- Try creating a broom for a special occasion, such as a wedding ceremony, welcoming a new life into the world, or even as a memorial to someone who has entered the "Summerland" – the Wiccan afterlife.

Did you know that the humble broom is the only magickal tool to represent both the male (stick) and female (bristles) energies? This unique energy combination explains its popularity as part of a wedding ceremony and is the perfect reason to make it a part of your wider magickal repertoire.

✦ LEGENDS OF THE BROOM ✦

Surprisingly, the first witch to confess to riding a besom was a man named Guillaume Edelin. By the time he "confessed" (under torture) in 1453, the image of a witch on a broomstick was already part of popular folklore.

The idea of flying on a broom is likely to have come from pagan fertility rituals in pre-Christian times, according to anthologist Robin Skelton. In his book, *The Practice of Witchcraft Today*, he discusses how under the light of the full moon, pagans rode on besoms or pitchforks like a hobby horse to encourage their crops to grow. Over time it seems the sight of this "broomstick dance" became distorted with accounts of "witches" flying through the night to cause mischief.

In some African tribes, the men leave the house while the women are sweeping. It's rumoured that if the broom accidentally hits them, they could become impotent unless they grab the broom and bang it on the wall. They then have to strike the wall anywhere between three and seven times to break the curse, depending on their cultural tradition.

✦.✦ GRIMOIRE ✦•✦

"Grimoire" means a magickal textbook of sorcery and craft. It originates from the French *grammaire*, meaning grammar, a word that used to refer to ancient and learned books written in Latin.

In a grimoire, one might find recipes and instructions for spells, along with rituals and use of magickal tools. It might also cover how to make your own protective talisman or work with supernatural entities such as angels, spirits, deities and demons. Grimoires are also said to hold magickal powers themselves.

Famous grimoires
- Francis Barrett, *The Magus – A Complete System of Occult Philosophy* (1801)
- Samuel Liddell MacGregor Mathers, *The Key of Solomon the King* (1888)
- Gerald Gardner, *The Gardnerian Book of Shadows* (1950s)
- Honorius of Thebes, *The Sworn Book of Honorius* (date unknown)

Many modern magicians create their own grimoires or Book of Shadows, journalling their own magickal rituals and experiences. Pick a beautiful book and get inspired!

✦.✦ ALTAR ✦•✦

Altars are used in religions worldwide as a centralized focus of worship and devotion. They're a specially designated place where religious rituals can be performed.

In magick, your altar can be used as a workspace for spell-casting and manifesting, and on the practical side, it essentially provides a table for holding your ritual tools.

It can be set up anywhere you have space; it could be a hearth, a table, bookshelf or dresser. When you create an altar, you're telling the universe that *this* is where the magick happens!

You can decorate your altar with different tools and symbols, such as your wand, the pentagram, crystals, statues of deities, flowers, candles, or representations of the four elements (earth, air, fire and water). You could even change the decoration of your altar to reflect the changing seasons and their relevant deities.

Remember to take care when burning candles or incense, and consider cleansing your altar of negative energy before starting any magickal rituals. You could do this, for example, by smudging it with sage (see pages 24 and 25).

✦ CANDLES ✦

Who doesn't love a candle for the feeling of peace and solace that it brings to the home and the spirit? The candle's flame represents spiritual purity and the infinity of the human soul, and working with them is one of the oldest and most common magickal arts.

While focusing on the flame can help you to channel your intentions and manifest your desires, candles can also be used for meditation, divinations, spells and rituals or in feng shui to energize the atmosphere of a room. There are even candles that harmonize with your astrological sign!

When choosing candles for a magickal practice, take time to think about the colour, scent and type of candle that will best enhance your work.

Depending on the spell, you may wish to use the following coloured candles:

- **Black** – healing, banishing negativity
- **Yellow** – happiness and success
- **Blue** – protection, peace
- **Orange** – positivity, courage
- **Green** – luck, healing, fertility
- **Red** – romance, passion, strength
- **White** – protection, truth, peace
- **Pink** – friendship

✦ CRYSTALS ✦

These beautiful natural rocks are enjoying a renewed popularity for the special gifts they bring. They've been here since the dawn of civilization, appreciated by cultures worldwide for their magickal healing properties. They've been used in religious rituals, worn as protective amulets and used as ornamentation on magickal wands. In modern witchcraft, crystals are used in meditation, divination and spell work.

Always cleanse your crystal first to remove negative energies. You can smudge it with some burning sage or give it access to sunlight or moonlight for a few hours. Next, charge it with magickal intention: visualize your goal while holding it in your hands and tuning in to its energy.

Here are some popular crystals and their associated specialities:

- **Amethyst** – aids peaceful sleep, calms and cleanses a space
- **Clear Quartz** – a master healer at all levels; brings clarity
- **Citrine** – "the merchant's stone" is associated with increased prosperity
- **Carnelian** – sparks motivation, fire and courage
- **Rose Quartz** – promotes unconditional love

Choose your crystal to match your intention and allow the magick to do the rest!

✦ ⋅ ✳ HERBS ✦ •✦

From adding them to your dinner to casting a spell, herbs have been prized for millennia for both their medicinal purposes and magickal qualities. Ancient herbalists were trusted to brew potions and use their knowledge of herbs to increase the potency of spells and rituals. They can be burned to cleanse magickal items and one's own energy, and having them around the home is believed to offer protection, dissolve negative energy and promote well-being.

Here are some common herbs and their uses:

- **Sage** – clears negative energies; often used in smudging, a smoke-cleansing ritual that involves burning dried herbs
- **Frankincense** – facilitates success, wealth, protection
- **Bay leaves** – aid in prophecy and divination
- **Pink rose buds** – used for spells of friendship and true love. Scatter these on your altar when casting love spells
- **Lavender** – promotes peace, calm sleep
- **Sandalwood** – cleanses and blesses a space, creates sanctity and harmony

As with any form of magickal tool, it's your intention that counts, so matching the herb to your intention adds power.

✦.✦ CHALICE ✦✦

A chalice is simply an elegant, ornate cup, and some people might be familiar with it already in Christian or Catholic rituals, where it's sometimes filled with wine symbolizing the blood of Christ. However, it was also a feature of pre-Christian times, and is still used today by many neopagans and Wiccans to drink from during rituals.

How you like your chalice is up to you; you may adore something glittering and jewel-encrusted or prefer something more simple. In paganism and neopaganism, a silver chalice is often chosen as it's said to represent moonlight and the moon goddess.

The chalice is also symbolic of abundance, fertility and the womb of the goddess. As it's aligned with the element of water, it's usually placed on the west of the altar.

If used at a coven meeting in witchcraft, Wicca or as part of a pagan or neopagan group ritual, towards the end of the ceremony the wine or water in the chalice is blessed and passed around between members to symbolize unity while enjoying the blessing of the goddess.

✦ ATHAME ✦

While the chalice is linked with feminine energy, the athame, a ceremonial knife, represents the masculine dynamic.

Thelemites, Wiccans and members of the Hermetic Order of the Golden Dawn (a secret occult society popular during the late nineteenth and early twentieth centuries) often work with both. Wiccans observe a ritual called the Great Rite, which represents the union of the god and goddess. The athame is placed into the chalice while the god and goddess are called upon in a gesture symbolizing the union of male and female.

The athame is a double-edged blade purely used for directing energy. It's never used for cutting and is not kept sharp. Its function is to cast a protective circle at the beginning of rituals, banish negative energies or summon the elements (see pages 33–36).

The athame is not mentioned in historic European witchcraft texts, but it's thought that the founder of Wicca, Gerald Gardner, learned of a ritual weapon called the *kris* during his time as a civil servant in Malaysia. Locally, it was said to be a magickal instrument, possessed of a *hantu* or spirit. Introducing a version of this to Wicca is one of Gardner's most fundamental contributions to modern magickal practice.

✦·✦ MAGICKAL SYMBOLS AND SIGNS ✦·✦

Since time began, humans have worked with protective signs and symbols to ward off evil and misfortune. You can use them in spell-casting, or wear as charms on a bracelet or necklace.

In the subsequent pages we'll explore eight powerful magickal symbols, also known as sigils.

Triquetra

Used by pagans and Celtic Christians, the Celtic shield, or triquetra, is a circle and a three-cornered knot. The knot represents the Triple Moon Goddess or Holy Trinity, while both the circle and the knot refer to infinity and protection that cannot be broken.

Crossed spears

Deriving from folk magick traditions, crossed spears could also be a simple drawing of axes, swords or hammers. When you see this, don't cross the bearer! In magick, the emblem blocks the actions or psychic intentions of an adversary.

Eye of Horus

This ancient Egyptian sigil signifies healing, knowledge and protection from evil. Named after the Egyptian god of the sky, Horus, it can also represent the "third eye", referring to heightened spiritual awareness. The use of eyes as symbolism is still used in many cultures around the world (such as the "evil eye" and the Eye of Providence), which all derive from the Eye of Horus. In most cultures it means spiritual guidance, divine blessing and protection.

Hamsa

In the Middle East and Africa, the eye of the Hamsa is protective, while the open right hand symbolizes power and blessings. It's worn or displayed as a charm against misfortune and poverty. In modern witchcraft the palm is protective, and the fingers symbolize the five blessings of love, wealth, health, wisdom and power.

Pentacle (or pentagram)

The five-pointed star is worn by Wiccans and pagans to symbolize faith and provide protection. Early occultists saw this as symbolizing the human being, and Leonardo da Vinci's *Vitruvian Man* is a human body drawn as a pentagram. Contemporary pagans believe the symbol represents the five elements (earth, air, fire, water and spirit) while the circle surrounding the star shows infinity and the body's energy field. Witches draw pentagrams in the air to create a sacred space or banish bad spirits.

Seal of Solomon

Composed of two interlaced triangles (rather than two overlapped triangles, which is a Star of David), this sigil is named after the Bible's King Solomon, who wore a signet ring with a hexagram seal. The interwoven hexagram design was said to represent the authority of God and to offer the wearer protection from evil.

Mars

Astrologers and alchemists originally created this sigil to symbolize the planet Mars. Named for the Roman god of war, in magick it equals conflict, personal power and virility. Work with this powerful sigil to bring warrior energy to hexes, curses and the repelling of nasty unwanted energies.

Solar cross

This prehistoric sigil dates back to Stone Age carvings. It symbolizes the light and movement of the sun as well as protection and the guardians of the four directions. Many later religious symbols, including the Christian cross, originate from this simple picture. Meditate on the cross's intersection to feel centred and calm when anxious, or to banish negativity.

THE HORNED GOD AND TRIPLE GODDESS

Important in the Wiccan and other pagan/neopagan faiths is the worship and union of the divine masculine and feminine. The cycle of the seasons and the death and rebirth cycles of the god and goddess shape the magickal year.

The Horned God

Based on the pre-Christian deities Cernunnos, Pan, Herne, Dionysus, the Oak King, the Green Man and the Holly King, among others, the two horns of the Horned God show his dual nature, representing both light and darkness and the union of the divine and the animal. He presides over the forest kingdom and symbolizes virility and the hunt.

The Triple Goddess

The Triple Goddess takes three forms: the maiden, mother and crone. Each form is aligned with a different phase of the lunar cycle. She is related to Hecate, Diana and Qudshu-Astarte-Anat, among others in pre-Christian mythology.

✦.✱ THE FOUR ELEMENTS ✱•✦

Magicians revere and are guided by nature. They often work with the seasons and four elements as well as the sun, moon and other natural things like herbs and crystals to strengthen their spell-casting. Mastering the elements is said to bring the external (the natural world) and the internal (our inner existence) into harmony.

In the fifth century BCE, the Greek philosopher Empedocles described the basic elements of air, fire, water and earth as the root of all existing matter. They've been seen as the foundation of magick ever since. This theory has passed through Qabalah and grimoire practices into modern traditions of ceremonial magick and paganism. Some magicians also work with elemental beings (nature spirits) such as sylphs (air), salamanders (fire), undines (water) and gnomes (earth).

Each element is associated with a cardinal direction – north, south, east or west – and has its own energy and symbol. The symbols represent the element's properties and powers as well as its physical aspect.

The directional associations on the following pages are for the northern hemisphere. For readers in the southern hemisphere, earth is associated with south, air with west, fire with north and water with east.

Earth

Earth represents the material world and the body. Fertile, nurturing and stable, this feminine element is associated with goddess power. The earth endures and flexes her strength. Earth is related to the pentacles suit in the tarot and connects with the direction of north.

Air

Air governs knowledge, action and change and connects to the soul and the breath of life. Focus on working with air if your magick relates to communication, wisdom or the powers of the mind. Allow air to float your troubles away or carry positive thoughts to others.

Air is the masculine element of the east and links to the suit of swords in tarot.

Fire

This masculine energy signifies passion, energy and sexuality, as well as purification. Just as the phoenix rises from the flame, fire both destroys and creates new life. Its energy is associated with the south, and in tarot it's related to the suit of wands.

Water

The feminine water element is connected with goddess energy and is the symbol of emotion, intuition, healing and cleansing. Associated with the direction of west, in some Wiccan covens, consecrated water (water given a blessing or invocation during a ceremony) is used to sanctify a cast circle. The corresponding tarot suit is cups.

✦.✶ THE FIFTH ELEMENT ✶•✦

Some modern pagan traditions work with a fifth element of spirit (also called the *aether*, or the *akasha* in Hindu philosophy) that is said to unify all the other elements. Spirit is the bridge between the physical and spiritual dimensions.

In Homeric Greek, *aether* means "pure, fresh air" or "clear sky", and Einstein thought that it occupied the space between all objects. While he could not assign it any physical properties (although some call it celestial energy), his idea fed into the theories of relativity, wave theory and dark matter. In Greek mythology, *aether* represents the pure space where the gods lived and the pure essence that they breathed.

The symbolic meanings of spirit in magick include transformation, alchemical processes, divine intervention, energy in motion and the eternal nature of life. Spirit represents the centre of a compass.

✦ THE MOON ✦

The moon has always held a unique fascination for magicians. They believe it has a special energy that can enhance their practice, and many cast their spells depending on which phase the moon is in, as each stage is thought to have its own specific energy. The moon is seen as a soft, feminine, receptive force. Marrying up your intentions with the lunar cycle can add potency to your spell-casting.

Here are some typical meanings associated with the lunar cycle:

- **New moon** – new beginnings and positive change
- **Waxing moon** – any area relating to growth, for example, abundance
- **Full moon** – the most powerful time for magick, with the moon's energy at its strongest
- **Waning moon** – letting go of things that no longer serve you, including clearing out unwanted negative energies
- **Dark moon** – introspection and reflection
- **Lunar eclipse** – deflection of obstacles impeding your growth
- **Solar eclipse** – rebirth and renewal

✦ WORKING WITH ✦ MOON DEITIES

In some pagan and Wiccan traditions, magicians also work with a deity, as well as a moon phase, for extra power. The lunar month is connected to the female menstrual cycle, and the moon's link with intuition and emotions also adds to its perception as a feminine energy. You may wish to call on one of the following moon goddesses in your practice:

- **Artemis** (classical Greek)
- **Coyolxauhqui** (Aztec)
- **Diana** (Roman)
- **Chang'e** (Chinese)
- **Ix Chel** (Mayan)
- **Mawu** or **Maou** (African, Dahomey)
- **Selene** or **Luna** (Greek)

Drawing down the moon
This beautiful Wiccan ritual is carried out under the light of the full moon and inside a cast circle by a coven's high priestess. (For more about casting a circle see page 96.) When a high priestess draws down the moon, she literally draws the goddess of the moon inside of herself. The goddess will then speak through her. The ritual can be held indoors or performed alone if preferred.

TRADITIONS AND CELEBRATIONS

Modern pagans, Wiccans and witches generally observe eight festivals throughout the year that follow nature's cycle. This cycle is called the Wheel of the Year, and each "sabbat" (holiday) marks either a main solar event (solstices and equinoxes) or the seasonal midpoints between them.

The timing of each celebration varies slightly, based on the lunar phase and geographic hemisphere. Below, the Wheel of the Year in the northern hemisphere is outlined, but some pagans in the southern hemisphere adjust these dates by six months to correspond with their own seasons.

Yule, Winter solstice
19–23 December

Also called midwinter, Yule marks the longest night (and shortest day) of the year and celebrates the rebirth of the sun. It's a time of new beginnings and transformation and the best time to ditch bad habits! This festival was celebrated in the British Isles long before the arrival of Christianity. However, there are similarities between Yule and Christmas traditions, such as exchanging gifts.

Imbolc
1 February
Imbolc celebrates the joyous coming of spring and symbolizes hope and renewed energy – a time for personal growth and some spring cleaning! Traditionally dedicated to Brigid, the goddess of healing, smithing and poetry, it's said to be the perfect time for witch initiations.

Ostara, Spring equinox
19–23 March
While Imbolc celebrates the beginning of spring, Ostara appreciates spring in full blossom: seeds being planted and trees and flowers blooming. This is a holiday of renewal and abundance, and eggs painted at this time symbolize new life, mirrored in the Christian tradition of Easter.

Beltane, or May Day
30 April–1 May
Beltane marks the beginning of summer, fertility and the flourishing of nature. May flowers, such as primrose, are used to decorate houses and animals, and for Wiccans, this sabbat represents love and romance as it's the time when the god and goddess are said to enter courtship.

Midsummer, or Litha, Summer solstice
19–23 June
Those long summer days are the peak of the solar year, with the pagan sun gods and goddesses basking in their full glory. The site of Stonehenge in the UK is famous worldwide for attracting thousands of druids and other pagan and neopagan groups each year to celebrate the summer and winter solstices.

Lughnasadh, or Lammas
1–2 August
The first harvest festival of the year, when the powers of the gods and goddesses begin to wane. Some pagans believe the Celtic Sun God Lugh pours his power into grain instead, and when it's harvested and baked into bread in his image, his life cycle is complete. Corn dollies are also made by Celtic pagans.

Mabon, Autumn equinox
20–24 September
The second harvest festival, when fruits and vegetables are harvested. The goddess evolves from mother to crone, and thanks is given for a successful harvest. It is also known as Harvest Home, and to modern druids as Alban Elued ("light of the water").

Samhain, or Hallowe'en
31 October–1 November

Though Wicca's Gerald Gardner referred to this sabbat as Hallowe'en, many pagans prefer Samhain to distance themselves from the commercialism of Hallowe'en.

Samhain marks the return of winter and a thinning of the veil between worlds, making it the ideal time to communicate with the dead – and one of the most powerful nights to do magick!

Also known as the final harvest, it's a time to honour ancestors, ask for their guidance, give thanks and set intentions as the turning of the wheel begins again.

A BRIEF HISTORY
OF MAGICK

Magick has been around as long as humans have! It's been practised in all parts of the world in many different forms and traditions throughout history.

In ancient civilizations, it was associated with religious or spiritual rites, forming part of a culture's perspective on the world, providing familiar rituals and a framework through which individuals could organize their lives.

During the nineteenth century, the development of stage magic and illusion complicated matters. Unscrupulous fortune tellers and fake mediums gave supernatural practices a bad reputation. The ancient word "magic" began to branch off into having a different meaning, and we now use it to refer to entertainment and illusion.

While the word "magick" is a modern one, the concepts it covers are ancient, such as those associated with paganistic rituals, shamanism and witchcraft. This chapter will look at the history of magick throughout the world, from its origins in ancient times through to present-day interpretations.

✦·✦ MAGICK IN THE ANCIENT ✦·✦ WORLD (3000 BCE–650 CE)

The Greek *magoi* gave us "magic", the original root word of magick. This term was used by the Median tribe of Persia and their Zoroastrian religion.

The classical world was fascinated by ancient Middle Eastern beliefs, so many of their magickal traditions originated from there. They were particularly obsessed with protecting themselves from sorcery, and there are written records of spells cast by sorcerers from both ancient Mesopotamia (modern-day Iraq) and Egypt. They addressed spells to elements, such as fire, and the earth's natural bounty, such as salt and grain, and, of course, to gods.

In Greco-Egyptian papyri ranging from the first to the fourth century CE, magickal recipes using animal ingredients are described, as well as ritualistic steps to ensure the success of the spell. Antique texts also reveal that the Greeks, Romans, Egyptians, Babylonians, Etruscans and Assyrians practised necromancy (rousing the spirits of the dead) to combat evil.

MAGICK AND DEITIES
✦ IN ANCIENT EGYPT ✦
(3100–332 BCE)

The ancient Egyptians loved magick! They worshipped over 2,000 deities, using spells, rituals and ancient texts to connect with them. Although it was a deeply healing practice, magick could also be used to cause harm, such as placing a curse on someone.

Just like magicians today, the Egyptians believed that objects such as charms or wands could be infused with the energy of magick.

Here are just a few of the Egyptian deities linked with magick:

- **Heka** – The god of magick and medicine, Heka is the personification of magick itself! The ancient Egyptians believed that the supernatural force of magick, and therefore Heka, created the universe.
- **Shed** – Protective god who shielded people from harmful black magick, illness and attacks from wild animals.
- **Isis** – An excellent deity to work with when casting healing spells. She protected against snake bites and scorpion stings and escorted the dead into the afterlife.
- **Bes** – Protective deity alongside his female companion Beset. They were said to bring a household good fortune and protect mothers and children.

✦.✳ HELLENISTIC MAGICK ✳°✦

For 300 years after the death of Alexander the Great (323 BCE), Europe enjoyed the Hellenistic age. This lasted through the Roman conquest of Greece until 30 BCE when the Romans conquered Egypt. The mysterious art of magick was an essential part of Greco-Roman life, from curse tablets to spells and evil prayers, herbs and poisons, love potions and protective charms. It was practised by both male and female magicians and available to all areas of society.

The Hellenistic period produced an abundance of written magickal texts and traditions, combining the main beliefs of the time, and drawing from Greek, Greco-Egyptian, Roman and Jewish practices. This systemization gave us many of the magickal traditions we have today.

The doctrines of the Hellenistic religions are still followed by various Jewish, Christian and Muslim groups, while Hellenistic art and architecture continues to influence Christian and Jewish iconography and architecture. Major religious texts, such as the Jewish Talmud and the New Testament are examples of Hellenistic thought, in both form and content.

THE GRECO-ROMANS AND MAGICK

In the Greco-Roman world, for every good act of magick there existed a counter-magick to ward off negative actions. Amulets were commonly used to protect against curses. Precious stones were believed to be super effective for this, but charms could also be made of organic material, such as beetles.

There have been some astonishing magickal discoveries from this period. A magician's kit, complete with tools, was unearthed in Pergamon (modern-day Turkey), which was once a Greek state during the Hellenistic age. A bronze table and base was found, along with a dish, bronze nail, bronze rings and polished black stones. They were engraved with symbols, letters and the names of supernatural powers. By this time, magick was firmly established worldwide; however, the practices revealed in the texts are thought to be much older.

Twelfth century demons

Between the collapse of the Roman Empire (fifth century CE) and the Renaissance (fourteenth to seventeenth centuries), word spread among medieval Christians that miracles by pre-Christian deities had, in fact, been carried out by demons. So by the twelfth century, many thought magick involved demonic intervention, leading to a frenzy of fear and hysteria. Witches were eventually caught up in this crossfire (see pages 54–55).

However, the works of Islamic philosophers gained favour in Europe in the twelfth century and offered an alternate view. These philosophers wrote in favour of magickal practices linked with astral or celestial magick, relating to the hidden powers of the planets and stars. This was absorbed into traditions harnessing nature's unseen power in acts of natural magick.

CORPUS HERMETICUM

One of the greatest influences on Western esoteric and magickal tradition is the text *Corpus Hermeticum*, attributed to Hermes Trismegistus, a combination of the Greek god Hermes and the Egyptian god Thoth. It explores topics such as astrology along with other occult sciences.

Translated into Latin in 1460, during the Renaissance and Reformation periods, Hermeticism provided a palatable alternative option that was halfway between Christianity and paganism.

HERMETICISM AND THE RENAISSANCE

Marsilio Ficino, the translator of the *Corpus Hermeticum*, believed that the text contained the lost ancient wisdom entrusted to Adam in the Garden of Eden.

Renaissance Europe was hungry for the philosophy of Hermeticism, while the mystical Judaic practice Kabbalah also attracted renewed interest. Kabbalah is said to reveal the hidden traces of God in the universe, and Hermeticism and Kabbalah became linked.

These traditions influenced the English philosopher and mathematician John Dee (1527–1608/1609), who worked with angels and advised some of Europe's most powerful monarchs. Dee inspired the title character of Christopher Marlowe's play, *Doctor Faustus* (1604). Faustus experiments with the dark arts and damns himself for eternity.

Hermeticism described a universal theory that combined religion, philosophy and magickal practice into a coherent whole, but while Ficino, Dee and others protested that these practices were entirely natural, they still had to fight the continuing accusations of demonic worship.

However, fascination with the distant past during the Renaissance inspired a return to the knowledge and ideals of the Hellenistic period.

✦.✳ HERMETIC QABALAH ✳•✦

Kabbalah with a "K" refers to the original Jewish tradition; Christian Cabala starts with a "C", while the Western Hermetic tradition spells Qabalah with a "Q".

This Western esoteric tradition, blending Hermeticism and Kabbalah, is the foundation for the magickal societies we know today, such as the Hermetic Order of the Golden Dawn, Thelema and the Fellowship of the Rosy Cross. It's the predecessor to the neopagan and Wiccan movements.

Hermetic Qabalah derives its influences from Jewish Kabbalah, Egyptian, Hellenistic and ancient pagan religions, Western astrology, alchemy, angelic and tarot magick, tantra and Hermeticism. It was thought of as natural, "good" magick, rather than the "evil" magick of sorcery or witchcraft.

During the Age of Enlightenment, from around 1685, Hermeticism was no longer recognized by the Christian church, so a number of hermetic brotherhoods were secretly founded, and Hermetic Qabalah flourished. While magick was disapproved of in Judaic Kabbalah, it became a main feature of Non-Jewish Cabala and Western occult philosophy.

Rosicrucianism and esoteric branches of Freemasonry also taught Qabalah and divine magick, laying the foundations for modern esoteric organizations.

✦ .✴ ALCHEMY AND MAGICK ✴ᐧ✦

The medieval practice of alchemy (a precursor to modern-day chemistry) was adopted by Hermeticism. Alchemy was concerned with the magick of converting base metals into gold and the discovery of the elixirs of life and was considered an occult science.

Alchemy had been practised alongside magick for thousands of years by various cultures. The astronomical signs of the planets at one time doubled as alchemical symbols, until medieval persecution forced alchemists to create their own secret symbols.

In the early seventeenth century the Rosicrucians, a secret brotherhood that used alchemical symbolism, created a connection between alchemy and magick that has powerful resonances today. Alchemists' obsession with melting metals meant new chemical elements and compounds were discovered, and many of their techniques, such as distillation, are still used in chemistry.

Some also say that the ancient use of magickal alchemical symbols and rituals have spawned modern concepts relating to the power of the mind, such as manifestation and visualization.

Nineteenth century magick

The French magician Eliphas Levi (1810–1875) assigned Hebrew letters to tarot cards, fundamentally linking Jewish esotericism to Western magick. Levi also inspired the Hermetic Order of the Golden Dawn, which developed Hermetic Qabalah further, combining Qabalistic principles with Greek and Egyptian deities in a cohesive way. It integrated systems such as John Dee's Enochian system of angelic magic and some Eastern concepts (most notably from Hinduism and Buddhism). The Hermetic Order of the Golden Dawn follows the structure of a Masonic or Rosicrucian-type esoteric order.

Aleister Crowley, the most well-known advocate of Hermetic Magick, started as a member of the Hermetic Order of the Golden Dawn before forming his own religion, Thelema (see pages 58–59).

The rise of neopaganism

Neopaganism started in the late eighteenth/early nineteenth century and became popular in Western Europe and North America during the second half of the twentieth century. It describes multiple religions reviving European pre-Christian polytheistic religions. While there is an abundance of neopagan magickal groups today, Asatru is one example of a modern neopagan religious reconstruction, officially recognized in Iceland and based on ancient Norse beliefs and ecological awareness.

✦.✳ MODERN MAGICK ✳•✦

Today, there are a large number of diverse magickal groups all over the world, from witches to shamans.

After a traumatic history, it's now considered special to be a modern witch. Although nowadays they're immortalized on TV and in Hollywood, witches weren't always so popular.

In pre-Christian Europe, witchcraft was an innate way of life. Healers, pagans and wise men and women worked with the natural world and prayed to multiple deities. However, fear and hysteria about the devil in the medieval era led to witches erroneously being linked with malicious practice.

The *Malleus Maleficarum*, a guide for hunting and persecuting witches written by German clergyman Heinrich Kramer in 1486, perpetuated that witches were in league with Satan. Misconceptions in this book fuelled the Salem witch trials of 1692 and the associated European witch hunts of the sixteenth and seventeenth centuries. In Europe, an estimated 40,000–80,000 people were burned, drowned and hanged.

Thankfully the Age of Enlightenment in the seventeenth and eighteenth centuries brought about more rational thought.

The UK's "Witchcraft Laws" were finally repealed in 1951, allowing for the return and evolution of numerous ancient traditions. Retired British civil servant Gerald Gardner, credited as the father of modern witchcraft, published *Witchcraft Today* in 1954 and founded Wicca. In the 1960s and 70s, Wicca spread to other English-speaking countries, inspiring feminist and environmental movements.

In Britain, different movements developed. Gardnerians trace their lineage back to Gerald Gardner, while Alexandrians are followers of Alex and Maxine Sanders, who further developed Gardner's ideas. Hedge Witches tend to practise alone rather than joining a coven, while the Dianic Craft operates on feminist principles.

However, like many magickal traditions, these groups are fluid and hard to define. Some witches may call themselves pagan or druid rather than identifying as Wiccan. Or their practice may be entirely personal to them and they may wish to identify with nothing at all.

Secular witchcraft, where witches have no particular spiritual interest, is also flourishing. Millions worldwide today are practising witches, and self-empowerment is considered to be at the heart of modern witchcraft.

✦ WICCA ✦

Wicca has the largest following among modern pagan or neopagan groups and is mostly practised in the West. Most Wiccans identify as witches and are inspired by the pre-Christian religions of Europe, North Africa and Western Asia and even other polytheistic religions such as Hinduism.

Wiccan groups call themselves covens, a term also used in witchcraft. Covens are usually led by a high priest and a high priestess, and each will have between three and 13 members, with 13 considered to be the ideal number.

To join a coven, you must have an initiation ritual. Most covens are secretive about their initiation rites, but a member will only be admitted once they've undergone a period of study and mentorship with an experienced member and have demonstrated their commitment to the coven's vow of secrecy, beliefs and practices. Wiccans reject cursing, seeing it as unethical. The majority of covens welcome both women and men, although many Wiccans today operate as solitary practitioners.

The pentagram, or five-pointed star, is the main symbol of Wicca.

Wiccan beliefs and practices

Wicca doesn't have a leader or governing body, allowing it to be a flexible movement that accepts different beliefs and practices.

Gardner worshipped a mother goddess and a horned god, representing the divine masculine and feminine, believing both to be equal and intertwining deities created by an unknowable divinity. Other subsequent Wiccan groups have had different ideas, such as solely promoting goddess worship and embracing other deities from world mythologies.

Wiccans differ in whether the deities literally exist or are symbolic figureheads, but they consistently worship deities from pre-Christian Europe. Many believe in an afterlife called the Summerland.

WICCAN VAMPIRE SLAYERS

Wicca's growing public profile spawned a series of American films and TV shows, prompting a teenage Wiccan subculture during the 1990s and 2000s, with social media responsible for further teenage interest in the 2010s. Some practitioners felt their religion had been trivialized, and from the early 1990s onward, many rebranded themselves as "traditional" witches.

✦ ·✴ THELEMA ✦•✦

Thelema is a modern interpretation of magick devised by occultist Aleister Crowley. In 1904, Crowley wrote *The Book of the Law*, a prose poem that forms the main scripture for Thelemites. Crowley claimed that the book was dictated to him by Aiwass, a guardian angel, and believers are free to interpret the text as they wish. In *The Book of the Law*, Crowley sets out the basics of Thelema:

"Do what thou wilt shall be the whole of the law."
This encourages followers to live by one's own "true will".

"Love is the law. Law under will."
This describes the belief that everyone is united with his or her true will through love.

"Every man and every woman is a star."
This statement suggests that everyone has unique talents and potential, and that all should be free to seek out their true self.

The "great work" for Thelemites is to strive towards higher states of existence. This can be achieved by uniting with higher powers and embracing one's true will and ultimate purpose in life.

Thelemic deities

The three main deities in Thelema can be interpreted as either literal beings or archetypes. Nuit, Hadit and Ra-Hoor-Khuit have their origins in the Egyptian divinities Isis, Osiris and Horus.

CELEBRATIONS

- Thelemic New Year: feast for the "supreme ritual" (20 March)
- Three-day feast for the writing of *The Book of the Law* (8–10 April)
- Equinoxes and solstices: rituals of the elements and feasts of the times
- Spring equinox: feast for the equinox of the gods (19–23 March) – also celebrates the founding of Thelema

Thelemites also celebrate significant milestones:

- Feast for life – the birth of a child
- Feast for fire or feast for water – a boy or girl's coming-of-age
- Greater feast for death – memorial event when someone has passed

✦ THE GODDESS MOVEMENT ✦

Have you ever considered how the figureheads in Abrahamic religions (such as Christianity, Judaism, Islam) are male? The neopagan goddess movement gained popularity in the Western world during the 1970s as a divine way to redress the balance.

The hundreds of goddesses that are venerated today were known around 5,000 years ago, before religion became patriarchal. The movement celebrates divine feminine energy and honours the woman for her whole life cycle – not only as maiden, lover and mother but also as the old woman, or crone. This is a welcome antidote to a Western culture that casts aside the old woman as no longer useful.

Some women (and men, looking to connect with their feminine energy) find goddess worship hugely empowering. Beliefs and practices vary widely, with some believing the goddesses exist independently (or are all one goddess with many faces), while others are drawn by the movement's connection with nature. Goddess energy is said to be present in all creation, from the stars to the trees and oceans.

✦ ⋅ ✳ SHAMANISM ✳ ✦

Shamans – sometimes called medicine men, seers or witch doctors – work with the soul and spirits of all types. Often associated with Indigenous and tribal societies, practices vary depending on culture, but shamanism has its roots in the earliest civilizations of far northern Europe and Siberia. Shamans are both celebrated and feared, and various scholars argue that numerous magickal rites carried out in other societies have derived from shamanistic practices.

Shamans work with nature spirits, such as rocks, trees and land, and animal and human spirits and ancestors. They're believed to heal the earth, communicate with spirits, heal the sick and guide the souls of the dead to the afterlife. Shamans can offer healing by removing misplaced energy (shamanic extraction) or returning the part of your soul to you that has been lost through trauma (soul retrieval).

Many shamans perform something called journeying as part of their practice. This is when they allow their soul to leave their body to roam other spiritual realms. They enter a "trance state" encouraged by the rhythmic beating of drums or rattles.

✦ VODOU ✦

Known as Voodoo in the Western world, this monotheistic religion from Africa is often linked to black magick. Misrepresentation in Hollywood, along with historical distortions of the religion, have erroneously led to Vodou being linked with torture, devil worship and even cannibalism.

In fact Vodou was influenced by displaced slaves who brought their traditions and religious practices with them, seeking a common spiritual identity. Forbidden to practise their beliefs, they merged their god with Catholic saints as a way to gain acceptability, leading to a blend of Catholicism, Western and Central African spirituality. A unique set of rituals formed over time, such as the use of dolls (poppets) and symbolic drawings.

Vodou is the only traditional African religion to have endured. It's still practised today in Benin, Togo, Haiti, Nigeria, Ghana, New Orleans and other places in the Caribbean, and is based on working with natural and supernatural forces and communing with ancestral spirits and patron saints.

Vodou rituals and practices

There is no standardization in Vodou, so practices vary widely. However, some of the most common are:

- **Spirit possession** – An important but often misunderstood element of Vodou worship, the lwa (great communal spirits) are commonly asked to possess a believer during a ritual. This is so that the community might speak to them and receive answers to any pressing questions.

- **Animal sacrifice** – Rituals can involve animals being killed, to provide food for the participants, but also to provide spiritual nourishment for the lwa. Food and other items are offered to the lwa as a sign of gratitude for their support.

- **Veves** – These are symbols drawn with cornmeal or another kind of powder. Each lwa has its own symbol, although some are linked to multiple symbols.

- **Voodoo dolls** – The common perception of sticking pins into Voodoo dolls is an unrealistic one. Followers of Vodou (Vodouisants) dedicate dolls to particular lwa to curry favour with them.

✦.✳ MAGICKAL CATS ✦✳✦

The cat has been associated with magick since ancient times. It's said that these mystical creatures can access the spiritual realm more easily than any other animal, and they were held so sacred by the ancient Egyptians that killing one was punishable by death.

The furry felines were associated with the Egyptian goddesses Bastet and Sekhmet, and the Norse goddess Freyja is said to have driven a chariot pulled by a pair of black cats.

In medieval times the cat became associated with witches, due to the ancient pagan fondness for them. Witches, it was believed, could take on a cat's form or inhabit their feline's body to carry out magick. As cats are naturally nocturnal creatures, people also associated them with the moon.

In modern witchcraft, the cat as a familiar (magical pet or helper), brings good fortune to its magickal owner and is said to protect them at night as they travel the spiritual realms in their sleep. Cats are also used for divination (see page 101). Many magickal practitioners have reported cats showing up when they're about to carry out magickal activities. In neopagan traditions, cats have frequently been said to make themselves comfortable in magickally designated areas, such as circles, grids or altars.

In Japan, the *maneki-neko*, "beckoning" or "happy cat", is used in feng shui layouts. Most of us are familiar with this beautifully decorated waving cat, now a frequent sight in shops and homes in the West. The *maneki-neko* is said to invite good luck into your home. He raises his paw in welcome, but this upraised paw also attracts wealth and fortune, while the fixed paw resting next to the body helps the homeowner to keep it.

- During the Renaissance era in the UK (circa 1485–1603 CE), guests could ensure a pleasant visit by paying homage to the family cat and kissing it on arrival!

- In rural Italy, good luck is said to be coming your way if you hear a cat sneeze!

✦ DRUIDRY AND NEO-DRUIDISM ✦

Druidry, or druidism, is a spiritual or religious movement that reveres nature and honourable relationships with others. Originally, a druid was a member of the high-ranking priestly class in ancient Iron Age cultures. From the Celtic meaning "oak knower", they were first mentioned in 40–50 BCE when Julius Caesar wrote about the Celtic priesthood. However, druidry declined with the rise of Christianity, and although druids were literate, they were forbidden to write down their hymns and practices.

The World Druidry Survey of 2018–2020 provided the first global study of modern druidry (neo-druidism), revealing that druidism is active in 34 countries. Neo-druidism is described as "a contemporary, nature-based, new religious movement". Neo-druids celebrate seasonal festivals, and practices include nature connection, sacred listening and reciprocity to allow druids to cultivate honourable relationships with both human and non-human beings.

The best known neo-druidic organization is the Order of Bards, Ovates and Druids, founded in the UK in the 1960s, with over 20,000 members worldwide. Unearth your inner druid by practising Celtic forms of divination, along with other magickal rituals!

THE TYPES
OF MAGICK

A young German nobleman, Heinrich Cornelius Agrippa von Nettersheim, defined three types of magick in the most widely known book on the subject, *De Occulta Philosophia* (*Three Books of Occult Philosophy*). Written in 1533, he generally identified magick as being ceremonial, celestial or natural.

- **Ceremonial magick** involves forms of divine tradition, such as rituals, and is carried out in the presence of an appropriate figurehead, such as a priest, priestess or shaman.

- **Celestial magick** exists where the earth meets the cosmos, such as astrology.

- **Natural magick** is practised through working with nature's resources, such as herbs, crystals and candles.

Today, with the expansion of magickal practice and a rise in practitioners, there are more categories than ever before. This chapter looks at white magick, black magick, herbalism, divination and clairvoyance, as well as ancient sub-categories of magick such as "high" and "low" magick, and emerging sub-categories, such as art magick. The boundaries between types of magick are often blurred, but what they all have in common is the sense of supernatural power that is believed to flow through the practitioner.

✦ SUB-CATEGORIES OF MAGICK ✦

Each type of magick has its own set of rules, rituals and practices, defined by tradition and culture. However, they often overlap. You may decide to try a few of these methods to see what you find yourself drawn to!

High magick
(ceremonial, learned or ritualized magick)
Some make a distinction between the "high" magick of the intellectual elite, and the "low" magick derived from common folk practices.

High magick is ritualized, formal, elaborate and exact, and its practitioners work with science-based forms of magick, such as astrology, numerology and symbols. They're interested in seeking enlightenment and spiritual growth.

Low magick
(also called "earth magick" or "folk magick")
Low magick thrives on spontaneity, creativity and instinct and often falls under the category of witchcraft. Many folk magick practices were passed down by word of mouth in families from ancient times. It tends to involve natural magick (herbs, animal spirits, earth energies), charms, symbols such as hex signs to ward off evil, or reciting healing chants over a wound.

Divinatory magick

Lots of people enjoy the many varied tools of divination, such as tarot cards, pendulums, scrying or the *I Ching*, and all types of magick can be involved here. These tools can be helpful in allowing you to understand where you are now and where your life path might lead. This could enable you to change course or feel positive that you're going in the right direction.

Sympathetic magick

This involves using an object (such as a doll or "poppet") as the focus of your intention. The object and the person you're placing your focus on become linked, and the items then carry the same energy so that when something happens to the object, it happens to the person. Most people will recognize the Voodoo doll as an example of sympathetic magick, and while it has a bad rap due to films and fiction, it is often used for good, to bestow healing or love on another.

If you don't fancy linking up your teddy bear, you could use a photo of someone or an object of theirs, such as a lock of hair.

Talismanic magick

This is the ancient practice of creating and wearing an object that has been "charmed", or given a particular intention, such as to protect the wearer and repel negative energies. The evil eye is a good example. Link your talisman with its desired outcome - for example, a heart necklace could be used to attract love.

Elemental magick

Incorporate the four main elements of earth, air, fire and water (and for Wiccans, the fifth element of spirit) into your rituals and spells. You can use objects that symbolize these elements (such as a lit candle for fire) or be aware of them in other magickal practices, such as divination. For example, tarot cards or crystals have associations with a specific element.

Petition magick

A sort of prayer magick, use this technique by asking a higher power to help you with a specific outcome. You may wish to use a ritual or set of rituals, or be spontaneous in your requests.

Chaos magick

An emerging form of magick, this involves forced manifestation using willpower. Magicians enter gnosis, a meditative state, to alter consciousness to change the energy of the world around them and manifest the results in reality.

Cosmic and planetary magick

Practised by astrologers and lunar witches, planetary magic is unknowable and vast, like the universe itself! A cosmic magician may act while planets are in a particular alignment to enhance rituals or work with the energy of cosmic entities.

Art magick

In this imaginative way to use magick, you can mix your creativity with the expression of your intentions and desires. Making the art can be ritualistic, with an outcome that could be healing, or manifesting something you'd like to appear in reality.

Other types may include (but are not limited to) green and plant magick, lunar magick, candle magick and sigil magick.

✦.✳ BLACK MAGICK ✳•✦

Black magick has the reputation of being used for ill purposes and is often associated with the devil or summoning of other evil spirits.

WHAT BLACK MAGICK IS USED FOR

- To cast a love spell over another and draw them to you

- To cast a binding spell to stop someone from harming you

- To raise spirits or communicate with the dead

Black magick is carried out by:

- Using magickal rituals, such as spells, chanting, etc. A "circle of power" (pentacle) is often involved, along with magickal tools and "words of power" relevant to the desired outcome, repeated three times.

- Placing a curse or hex on someone to control them or bring them bad luck.

BLACK MAGICK AND RELIGION

Black magick has always been intertwined with religion and sacred rituals. *Magic and Alchemy* by Robert M. Place (2009) traces both black and white magick back to the primitive and ritualistic worship of spirits.

Place equates shamanic possession with white magic, while the kind of traditions that developed into modern black magick involved working with the same spirits, but manipulated by the practitioner for their own gain.

Many modern Wiccans, witches and magicians are at pains to distance themselves from the concept of black magick. The rise of self-help spiritualism and new-age beliefs are based on benevolent magick and beliefs of love and kindness.

Black magick and Hinduism

Lord Shiva (also known as the destroyer) is linked to black magick in ancient Hinduism. Working with him is said to assist the practitioner with darker powers, such as overpowering your enemy. Black magickal practices can be used to defeat another by driving them away or causing problems in their lives, or by blocking the flow of energy in an opponent's body.

NECROMANCY
✦ (OR "DEATH MAGICK") ✦

Deriving from the Greek *nekros* (dead body) and *manteia* (divination), necromancy is considered a form of black magick or sorcery. It involves raising the spirits of the dead to divine information. Necromancers may be looking for answers to secrets, such as where the deceased may have buried some money, or even the name of a murderer. It can be used for positive purposes, such as relaying forgiveness from an ancestor to a living relative.

A popular pastime among the Assyrians, Babylonians, Egyptians, Greeks and Romans, in medieval Europe necromancy was condemned by the church, which did not look upon it so liberally. Thus, it came to be associated with black magick.

> Ancient magicians would work within a consecrated circle in a graveyard to ward off the anger of the dead as they carried out their necromantic practice. It's said that a spirit who'd died prematurely or violently still had unused vitality in their body – so body parts of corpses were used as ingredients or charms in some ancient witchcraft practices!

✦ CHINESE BLACK MAGICK ✦

Known as *gu* (meaning poison) or *jincan* (meaning golden silkworm), this practice of venom-based poison, mainly from the south, is entrenched in Chinese folklore. Although it's still rumoured to exist today, it's said to have been used in ancient times to harm others.

Gu magick was rumoured to cause sickness, harm and even death, control someone's will or confuse and seduce, resulting in a demonic sexual appetite.

To prepare the poisonous potion, creatures such as snakes and scorpions were sealed into a container, where they would eat each other. These animals were known as "golden silkworms", alleged to produce gold if the right sacrifices were made to them.

The remaining survivor of this deadly showdown would have accumulated all the toxic substances of the others, and its poison could then be administered discreetly to an enemy.

A grain-eating insect called the wug pest was also used for malicious purposes and released into an adversary's territory to destroy crops or stored food. It was also allegedly used by females who wanted to lure themselves a mate!

✦ ⋅ ✦ THE EVIL EYE ✦ ✦

Has anyone ever "given you the evil eye"? Or perhaps you yourself have given someone the *mal de ojo* ("bad eye" in Spanish). This ancient superstition is still commonly found around the Mediterranean and Aegean as well as in Latin America. In Arabic cultures it's known as *ayin harsha*, while in Italy, someone could give you the *malocchio* if they were displeased with you!

Someone giving you *that look* is said to cause harm merely by looking at you; the giver could be brimming with jealousy, or perhaps just a bit irritated with you! According to tradition, it is possible to give someone the evil eye unintentionally, but for those who do it intentionally, the evil eye is linked to witchcraft, sorcery and black magick.

In many cultures, protective amulets and charms are worn around the neck to ward off the evil eye, as well as certain magickal practices such as prayers or protective spells.

✦ WHITE MAGICK ✦

In contrast to black magick, white magick is used for healing, protection and other purposes, such as reaching higher states of consciousness. The practitioner works in league with "natural phenomena" and has only good intentions. Practitioners might be known by the title of healer, wise man or woman, white witch or wizard. Some believe they have magickal powers due to hereditary abilities or due to experiencing a supernatural event that awakened them to their talents.

As with all magick, practices vary significantly between belief systems (such as witchcraft) and individual practitioners but white magick is practised through healing, blessings, incantations, prayers, charms, actions and intentions.

According to Robert M. Place, modern white magick is founded on prehistoric shamanistic magick. It works to cure illness and assist well-being, interpreting dreams and the future, generating good luck, tracking down lost items, pacifying spirits or ancestors, or asking for good weather or a favourable harvest.

Gareth Knight, in his book *A History of White Magic* (1978), also suggests that white magick dates back to the earliest religions, including the traditions of ancient Egypt and, later, Judaism and early Christianity. He sees the creation of symbols combined with the ideas of these early religions practising "natural" magick, along with later philosophical thinking, culminating in the Western understanding of the practice.

Knight gives the example of the star as a white magick symbol. It's been hugely significant throughout history, from Judaism and early Christianity in the form of the Star of David through to Masonic custom and modern neopaganism. Neopagan groups, along with other white magick practitioners, currently work with the star shape in the form of the pentagram.

White magick is also associated with feminine concepts such as goddess worship and nature spirits. In modern fairy tales, the idea of white witchcraft is often associated with a kindly feminine presence, such as a grandmother or other motherly spirit.

Worship of Mother Earth and being at one with nature is also strongly linked to white magick practices.

✦.✳ DIVINATION ✳✦

The *Oxford English Dictionary* defines divination as "the practice of seeking knowledge of the future or the unknown by supernatural means". The word itself alludes to communion with the divine.

The word of the gods was divined in many ways in the ancient world. The Romans interpreted the behaviour of birds (*augury*) while the Etruscans read the entrails of sacrificed animals (*haruspicina*). Divination played a large role in political decisions and the right time to act, such as waging a successful war.

Nowadays, we'd recognize divination most in traditions such as astrology, tarot cards, dowsing and even the Ouija board. With the huge popularity of horoscopes, astrology - in multiple forms - is the most common form of divination today.

While the practice of divination is so old that it's hard to trace its origins, in the first century BCE, the Roman politician Cicero wrote a treatise called *De Divinatione* (*Concerning Divination*). In it, he draws a distinction between inductive, interpretive and intuitive forms.

Inductive divination

This type of divination relates to reading signs in mostly non-human phenomena, such as reading nature (e.g. flocks of birds) or the weather (e.g. lightning). These are seen as genuine signs from the divine, but signs such as reading falling arrows shot from a bow are also included.

In ancient Mesopotamia, they practised haruspicy, a type of inductive divination that involved reading livers and other animal entrails. Today, thankfully, we read palms instead!

Inductive divination sometimes overlaps with interpretive divination (see page 82) as some "natural" systems are interpreted by a professional diviner.

For example, the ancient Chinese practice of divining with tortoise shells was used during the Shang dynasty (c. 1600–1046 BCE). A fortune-teller would carve or paint symbols on the turtle shell or the shoulder blade of an ox before applying fire until the shell or bone cracked. They would then interpret the direction of the crack in relation to their symbols. Divining with oracle bones gave birth to the first recognizable Chinese script.

Interpretive divination

In interpretative divination, supernatural experiences combine with a human action. Perhaps you find an answer to the worry on your mind by opening a book at a random page, where the content seems to "speak" to your situation. Or you switch on the radio, only to hear a song that you associate with a particular person.

Interpretive divination mostly involves the reading of portents, omens or other phenomena, and it may overlap with the third type of divination: intuitive.

It can be dramatic, such as in divination by fire (pyromancy), or gentler, such as divination by water (hydromancy). In some trans-Saharan societies, the diviner may hold a seance around the fire to identify a culprit. It's said the fire will suddenly "explode" upon the accused – this is obviously very different to Western ideals of fair trial. In other places, pyromancy is carried out by throwing objects into the flames and reading the signs in the fire's reaction.

Hydromancy can range from reading the reflections in a shallow pool of water, to analyzing the movements of floating objects, such as tea leaves.

✦ ⊹ ✦ INTUITIVE DIVINATION ✦⁙✦

The most thrilling form of divination – this is where mediums and other "spiritual performers" come into their own! Supernatural phenomena combine with a human's intuition and their interpretative abilities.

Intuition is believed by some to involve some special skill or natural ability for spirit connection and relies on the power of the individual to receive knowledge, rather than placing the onus on the gods to impart it.

Intuitive divination may occur privately to an individual via spirits, visions or dreams, but a typical example of an intuitive diviner is a shaman, who uses trance states to connect with other realms and discover information. They can induce these states automatically or by ingesting a hallucinogenic drug such as ayahuasca. The shaman could also use autokinetic techniques that raise the energetic frequency for such a journey, such as beating drums and rattles, or hand trembling, which is practised among the Navajo.

Trance is associated with spirit possession and speaking as that spirit. Many diverse religious traditions worldwide, including Christianity, have been known to practise this form of divination, and it's still powerful in nomadic societies.

✦ · ✷ CLAIRVOYANCE ✷ᵒ ✦

The word "clairvoyance" probably conjures up images of a bejewelled lady leading a seance, but it describes an ability to see things with the "mind's eye". It could relate to someone's ability to see your future or detect energies or spirits.

Magickal practice involves sensing things beyond the boundaries of the physical world, things that are not visible to our naked eye, and clairvoyance is one of the ways to do this. In French, *clair* means "clear" and *voyance* means "vision". Many spiritual and religious practices throughout history have benefitted from this valued skill.

A clairvoyant uses their intuition and perception, drawing on their inner senses to receive images in their mind's eye, like a scene from a movie or a daydream. They then combine what they see with their intuition (and sometimes divinatory tools) to answer your burning question or build a picture of what could happen, based on the past and present.

Said to be a natural ability, what makes someone a clairvoyant is how they are able to enhance and strengthen their skills by practice.

✦ BECOMING A CLAIRVOYANT ✦

All of us are said to have a natural ability, but are you in tune with your psychic abilities? Here's how to tell if you're ready to harness your clairvoyant skills:

- You have super vivid dreams that seem real... and you can remember them in detail when you wake up. You may find yourself having the same dream over and over, so perhaps it's time to wake up and take notice!

- If you ever experience a tingling feeling in the middle of your forehead, between your eyebrows, you might be feeling your third eye becoming active.

- Perhaps you sometimes see images, symbols and visions in your head. This could happen while you're awake, or while you're busy slumbering. What are they trying to tell you?

- Have you ever seen something out of the corner of your eye? This may make you do a double-take, to check whether you really did see something or not. Who knows?

✦ HONING YOUR ✦ CLAIRVOYANCE

As you learn the discipline of focus and concentration, clearing thoughts and opening your mind will help you identify any visions coming into your head. You'll need to see beyond your five senses, so meditation is a good place to start. If you can, meditate daily for 20–30 minutes until clear sight has become instinctive and automatic.

EXERCISES AND TIPS

- Don't be afraid to daydream and let your mind wander. See where it takes you!
- Connect with any spirit guides, gods, goddesses or other supernatural beings that you regularly work with.
- Practise giving readings.
- Meditate with a crystal that stimulates your third eye, such as lapis lazuli, sodalite, labradorite or moonstone. The third eye is where you'll receive images and visions.
- Keep a dream journal to help you understand the messages you're being given.

✦ .✴ HERBALISM ✴ ✦

An example of natural magick, there are no better tools for your craft than herbs, with more than 28,000 plant species used for medicinal purposes around the world.

Plants have been used for thousands of years in rituals and as food or medicines, and herbalism has been practised in cultures everywhere by healers, shamans, medicine women and witches.

In some ancient cultures, rituals and prayers were used alongside physical healing, with the patient undergoing smudging for cleansing, given a herbal tea to sip, and incantations to the spirits performed for a speedy recovery. As well as healing, plants were used in other areas of magick for talismans, potions and spells.

In modern times, witches continue to cast spells with herbs or make potions to heal the sick, while many neopagans also use herbs as part of regular ritual practice. Each plant offers its own specific properties, so from increasing your abundance to healing, there's a cornucopia of benefits that can enrich your life.

✦ USING HERBS ✦

Some plants can be toxic to animals and/or humans, so be careful to fully research the plants you're using first. If you're planning to ingest herbs in a tea or tincture, make sure they're safe to consume, and be aware that some herbs are contraindicated for specific medical conditions. Check with a professional if in doubt.

Hallucinogenic plants

Ayahuasca ceremonies have become increasingly trendy as spiritual seekers look to this hallucinogenic herb to offer them enlightenment or healing from trauma – however, this practice is controversial and considered by many to be potentially unsafe.

Ayahuasca is a drink brewed by a shaman from the *Banisteriopsis caapi* and *Psychotria viridis* plants. It leads to the drinker experiencing an altered level of consciousness due to the psychoactive substances in the plants. Ingested for spiritual and religious purposes by ancient Amazonian tribes, this hallucinogenic brew is still used by some religious communities in South America and can cause both positive and negative health effects.

Using herbs for divination

1. Crush some patchouli, wormwood or mugwort to a fine texture and spread evenly into a small square container made of ceramic or glass.

2. Eyes closed, gently touch the centre of the dish with the index finger of your non-dominant hand.

3. Move your finger around the dish, allowing it to draw as it wishes.

4. Remove your finger and open your eyes.

5. Have a good look at what you've just drawn or written in the herbs, and perhaps take a picture of it in case you can't make sense of it just yet! The meaning may occur to you later, and as you get more experienced, you'll be able to divine meanings more quickly.

Using herbs for protection

1. Bind the stems of a few protective herbs together, such as thistle, honeysuckle, hyssop and fennel.

2. Tie the stems together with some thread and hang them up in a suitable place.

3. Express your intention for what you wish to be protected.

✦.✲ USING HERBS FOR MAGICK ✲⋅✲

There are many ways to enhance your magickal intentions with herbs. Take inspiration from some of the following:

Teas or infusions

Enjoy your cuppa even more by understanding the extra benefits of a magickal brew! You can buy pre-made herbal teas in bags or make your own infusions with loose leaf tea and a strainer. Before infusing your herbs, remember to charge them by setting your magickal intention for how you want them to work. Then sit back and enjoy as you ruminate on your intention with each sip.

Bath

Infusions can be used as part of a comforting bath routine. You can pour a herbal tea directly into your bath water or try making a big tea bag out of muslin or hessian.

Charms

Make a little bag of selected herbs and place it around your house (for example, by the front door to protect your home), or carry it with you in a pocket. To make your own charm, place some herbs in a square piece of fabric, and then tie the ends with ribbon or string.

Poppets

Poppets are little fabric dolls with herbs sewn inside. They work best when you use them on yourself as they're perfect for healing and protection spells. You can buy ready-made poppets online or from specialist stores.

Powders

Break down the herbs with a mortar and pestle, thinking about the plant's magickal properties as you do so. Powders can add potency to spells and incantations.

Ointments

Melt a base ingredient (for example, an oil or cocoa butter) and add powdered herbs. As you work, imagine what you desire has already been manifested. While the ointment is warm, transfer it to an airtight container. Use on pulse points.

Oils

Soak fresh herbs in a base oil, such as almond, grapeseed or olive oil for several days, before straining them. Use for anointing or rituals.

Incense

The delightful aromatic scent of herbs can aid relaxation and concentration during meditation, rituals and ceremonies. Buy a favourite ready-made incense stick or burn some powdered herbs on a charcoal disc or in a little dish.

✦ PRACTICAL MAGICK ✦

The great news is that herb magick is very practical – you can work with the ingredients you already have in your kitchen!

Try any of the following for a bit of enchanted assistance:

- **Prosperity: Bay leaf** – looking for a new job? Write your desire on a bay leaf and place it in your pocket. Burning bay leaves in incense adds extra potency to money spells.

- **Friendship: Orange and lemon** – to strengthen friendships, use dried orange or lemon peels in a potpourri.

- **Love: Yarrow** – associated with Venus and Aphrodite, two goddesses of love, call on them for assistance while working this herb in to spells and rituals.

- **Courage: Cinnamon** – if you find yourself needing a boost of courage, tie a pair of cinnamon sticks together. Place under your bed or carry with you.

- **Intuition and Prophecy: Jasmine** – if you've got an important decision to make or you'd love some guidance from your dreams, burn some dried jasmine before bed to stir your intuition.

PRACTISING
MAGICK

Practising magick is using the power of your intention and will to manifest change in the physical world. There are many different ways to go about this – there's a whole multitude of amazing traditions and beliefs from all round the world to choose from!

Some examples you might be familiar with are spell-casting, palm-reading, astrology, manifestation, tarot and the *I Ching*, although there are so many other fascinating types of divination and spiritual practices.

It's best to prepare any tools you'll need in advance (see page 13), as well as preparing a space for your practice. Prepare your space by setting up an altar (if using one) appropriate to that day's theme, smudging an area with dried herbs, such as sage, to cleanse away any negative energies, and creating or casting a protective circle.

In this chapter we'll look at a selection of different magickal practices and how you can prepare for your session.

PREPARING FOR
MAGICKAL PRACTICE

- **Meditation** – if you can, meditate daily, starting small with just ten minutes a day. There are many different styles of meditation, for example, with breathwork or music, so explore what feels good to you. Meditation is a key discipline in magick, allowing the practitioner to feel grounded and helping the mind to become clear so that it can focus on pure intentions and be open to intuition.

- **Create a protective space** – some traditions create a protective circle for spell-casting or other magickal rituals, while others work with the pentagram or hexagram symbols for this purpose. Whichever you choose to work with, creating a safe space is crucial to your practice.

- **Record your experiences** – journal any rituals that you develop spontaneously along with any insights and revelations. This helps you to realize how far you've come and develop a deeper understanding of both yourself and magick. It's also useful to keep a dream journal; important insights can drop into our heads when we're at our most relaxed – such as having a snooze!

✦.✦ CASTING A MAGICK CIRCLE ✦°✦

There are many different ways of creating a sacred space. Wiccans and witches tend to cast a circle, protecting the magician from negative energies and adding power to the spell or manifestation.

Preparing your circle
1. First, draw the circle. This could be done physically, by marking it out using chalk, salt, or a rope or cord, or energetically, by visualizing a circle of light around yourself.

2. Cleanse the area by sweeping with a broom or smudging with burning herbs.

3. Choose something to represent each element, and place in the appropriate cardinal direction, either in the circle itself or on the four corners of an altar inside the circle.

4. Call on the elements to protect and balance the space, known as "calling in the quarters". You can call in the elements collectively or individually.

Suggestions for your magick circle:
- **North: Earth** – soil, salt, green candle
- **East: Air** – incense, yellow candle
- **South: Fire** – red candle, spices or spicy foods, red/orange gemstone
- **West: Water** – small dish of water, blue candle

✦ INVOKING AND BANISHING ✦ THE PENTAGRAM

Neopagans, Thelemites and the Hermetic Order of the Golden Dawn often work with the Lesser Ritual of the Pentagram, using a pentagram shape rather than a circle. They work with five elements (including the fifth element of spirit). After drawing a pentagram, they begin by clearing any negative energies or impurities in the elements. They then invoke the elements in their pure form, before inviting in the four main archangels, Michael, Uriel, Gabriel and Raphael.

Wiccans work with a pentacle – a pentagram enclosed within a circle.

Closing the space

When working within either a circle or pentagram, remember to clear or close the space at the end of your practice. You can do this by thanking the elements (and archangels) and telling them they can leave. You can release them as a group or, if you called in each element individually, dismiss them in the opposite direction to which you called them in from. For example, if you went anticlockwise to call them to your circle or pentagram, move clockwise to dismiss them.

✦ SPELL-CASTING ✦

Spell-casting is a fun, empowering and mystical part of magickal craft.

What is a spell?

- A **spell** is a way of directing your energy with magickal intention.

- An **incantation** is a spell created using words.

- Objects are not inherently magickal but help us to channel our energy.

The most successful spells are those that respond to a burning desire or need in your life. Bear in mind, however, that you should be in a peaceful and balanced state of mind before casting, as the outcome of your spell will reflect your emotional state at the time of creation. If you cast your spell while stressed or upset, you may get erratic results. To create a positive outcome, ensure that you channel your magickal energy with focus, compassion and wisdom.

✦.✶ SPELL-CASTING TIPS ✦˙✶

Repetition

Repeating your spell or incantation will help to reinforce your intention. The power of poetry is also said to be music to the universe's ears:

"You should know well,
that saying your incantation in rhyme
doubles the strength of your spell!"

Charging objects and ingredients

Some might argue that the only true ingredient you need in a spell is magickal intention, meaning that you can energetically charge any object. This could include charging a cooking pot for use as a cauldron or charging spices for use in infusions.

Location

When deciding where to perform an incantation, remember that physical thresholds such as doorways, windowsills and even cracks in the floorboards can become magickal portals. These are said to open the space between worlds. Complete the spell by closing any portal you open. You could do this simply by saying "goodbye" or asking the portal to close.

✦.✳ AUGURY ✳⁺✦

Have you ever noticed that little robin who sits outside your window every day?

Birds are magickal creatures said to bridge the gap between the physical world and the spiritual, carrying messages from the divine. Observing their behaviour is said to reveal the future. Dating back thousands of years, this was an early method of magick used by ancient Egyptians, Greeks, Romans, Celts and the Indigenous peoples of North America.

Think about the birds you see around you on a daily basis. Have you noticed an unusual bird that you don't normally see, or one that's behaving oddly? Perhaps you've seen a flock of birds in a strange shape (if so, think about what that shape might mean). Sometimes you may feel instinctively that you know what they're trying to say; an emotion or feeling of clarity about something may drop into your head at the moment that you see them. Always pay attention to anything that's on your mind when you notice a bird, as it could be carrying a message just for you!

✦ AILUROMANCY ✦

Ailuromancy is a form of divination carried out by reading a cat's behaviour.

Any unusual movements by your moggy may indicate bad weather or spiritual activity. If you've ever noticed your cat reacting to something invisible, they could be playing with your household spirits! According to Wiccan high priestess Doreen Valiente, cats enjoy seances and have been known to astral-project, meaning they can have intentional out-of-body experiences.

You may also have noticed how they like to sit right in the middle of a ritualistic space, perhaps climbing on an altar or wandering into a circle, especially while you're spell-casting! They'll want to get involved, so they'll just stroll in and make themselves comfy.

In the past, sailors often kept an eye on the ship's cat to predict the weather. A cat grooming its fur against the grain predicted hail or snow, while a sneeze foretold that a thunderstorm was on its way. In Colonial America, it was said that a cold snap was due if your cat sat with its back to the fire all day.

✦.✴ SCRYING ✴˙✦

For many of us, the Evil Queen's famous consultation of her mirror in *Snow White* is our first introduction to scrying, an ancient form of "seeing". Also known as hydromancy, oculomancy or crystal gazing, "scry" comes from the Middle English term "descry" and means "to reveal".

The practice seems to have first appeared in China around 3000 BCE, Egypt in 2500 BCE and Greece in 2000 BCE. However, the notorious French prophet Nostradamus (1503–1566) is considered the godfather of scrying. Using a method from ancient Greece, he did his scrying in a bowl filled with water.

Although we often associate it with predicting the future, the future is open to change, so it's more useful to think of it as a way of tuning in to your intuition and opening up to messages from the universe. Gazing into a reflective object can provide us with information through symbols and images, interpreted by the scryer into spiritual guidance, such as clarity on relationships or the potential outcomes of different choices.

Scrying tools

Scrying requires a light trance-like state. It can be carried out with a reflective surface, such as a crystal ball, obsidian mirror or water (using a scrying bowl, lake or pond) or a variety of mediums, such as tea leaves, coffee grounds, a candle flame, a log fire or wax. Other forms of scrying include cloud-gazing, smoke-reading and soul-gazing.

Simple scrying

Scrying was connected to the magick of the moon in ancient times, so most people practise after 10 p.m.

Try the following method:

1. Choose a scrying tool.

2. Find a quiet space and a comfortable position.

3. Close your eyes and achieve a light trance through meditation, awareness of the breath, the repetition of a mantra or another technique that stills the mind and relaxes the body.

4. Hold a soft, focused gaze on your scrying tool. Tune in to your intuition, trust it and be open to any images, symbols or moments of clarity.

✦ TAROT ✦

One of the most popular magickal practices of modern times, tarot is loved for the depth and nuance of information that it provides. People have been seeking comfort and guidance since long before the tarot's first official appearance, in northern Italy in the mid-fifteenth century.

In a reading, you select the cards that you feel drawn to, guided by your intuition or your spirit guides or deities. The cards are then interpreted by an experienced practitioner (you can also learn to read tarot for yourself or your friends).

The original Rider Waite tarot pack is the most popular worldwide. In it, there are 78 cards and four suits, giving guidance in different areas:

- **Wands** – business and enterprise
- **Cups** – matters of the heart
- **Pentacles** – finances
- **Swords** – struggle and conflict

You may wish to have a general reading or ask the tarot a particular question. Each card is associated with specific guidance and energy, meaning you can work with it in manifestation, or as a powerful magickal tool in spells and ritual work.

✦.✦ RUNES ✦˙✦

Rune casting is a divination system dating back to pre-Christian Scandinavia, where Norse and Germanic peoples practised ancient runic magick to seek answers to a problem. The Norse tribes believed that each rune had its own consciousness and energy, so it could be called upon like any god, spirit, angel or demon and used for blessing, protection, healing or cursing. They often consulted runes for the most advantageous time to travel or wage war.

Still used today, small stones or pieces of wood are inscribed with one of 24 ancient symbols. While meditating on a specific question, the caster draws out the rune stones from a small pouch and throws them at random. They will then interpret a reading, considering the pattern formed by the runes, as well as individual and collective meanings.

Modern systems of runic divination are based on traditions such as Hermeticism and the *I Ching*.

You can engrave a rune on wood or metal and wear it as a talisman for protection or to attract love or wealth. They can also be used to focus the intention of a spell, by inscribing the relevant rune on a candle or other magickal tool.

✦ DOWSING ✦

This ancient divination practice uses rods to detect energy currents, objects or spirits, although dowsing in its modern form is often carried out with a pendulum.

Dowsing rods

Dowsing rods are usually made from metal, although you can use Y-shaped branches of willow, rowan or hazel. When you hold the rods, they'll move when they detect energetic activity. You can use them to:

- Search for objects

- Detect underground water

- Cleanse a space to release spirits

- Pick up energetic vibrations, such as spirits or "ley lines"

Ley lines

These are supernatural energetic grid lines that are said to criss-cross the Earth, moving between multiple historic landmarks such as Stonehenge and St Michael's Mount. The Chinese call these dragon lines, while the Incas used spirit lines and the Irish have fairy paths.

In Australia, the Indigenous Aboriginal people have dreaming tracks or song-lines – paths that cross the land

and sky. The paths are chronicled through stories, painting, dance and traditional songs, enabling the Aboriginals to navigate Australia's vast deserts.

Dowsing with a pendulum

A pendulum is a chain that has a weighted object on it, often a crystal. The weighted object moves when you ask it a question, and will give a "yes", "no" or "don't know" answer. First, you'll need to find out how it wants to talk to you!

1. Hold the chain between your thumb and forefinger about 5-10 cm up the chain from the weighted object.

2. Holding it steady, ask "show me a yes".

3. Observe in which direction it swings.

4. Ask it to show you each a "no" and a "don't know".

5. Test these responses a few times by asking it a significant question you're sure of the answer to.

Depending on your belief, pendulums work by connecting with divine or magickal forces. Others put the swing down to involuntary muscle movements that channel the higher self, or the wisdom of the body.

You could also make your own pendulum using a chain and suitable weight, such as an ancestor's ring.

✦.✴ PALMISTRY ✴ˑ✧

This simple way of reading your own destiny can be carried out just by looking at your hands! Also known as chiromancy, the art of reading the patterns on your palms can help you gain insight into many different aspects of your life, such as behaviours, relationships, personality and life path.

Palmistry is believed to have originated in India, with its roots in Hindu astrology, the Chinese *I Ching* and Romani fortune tellers. It was even around in Greece during the time of Aristotle.

There are many ways you can read information, including looking at lines, mounds (or mounts), and the shape of your hands and fingers. In general, the dominant hand reveals information relating to the present and future, and the non-dominant hand tells all about your childhood, relationships, hopes and fears.

The three most important lines to read are:

- **Life line** – indicates health and well-being over the course of a lifetime

- **Head line** – details how a person thinks and acts

- **Heart line** – deals with relationships, passions and what drives a person

✦ ONEIROMANCY ✦

Did you know that dreams could be magickal? Every time you have a fearful dream, or indeed a pleasant one, be sure to notice any objects, symbols or themes that pop up, from hissing snakes to receiving that lovely gift! You may be receiving a clue from the spirit world about what might happen next.

Oneiromancy is a form of prophetic divination from dreams, revered in most ancient cultures and still recognized as important in modern times. The ancient Greeks, Egyptians and Babylonians believed that dreams were messages or warnings sent to the soul by gods or the dead. Diviners or seers in these ancient cultures had huge political and social influence and were often called upon to interpret the dreams of those in power.

The most famous example of oneiromancy is the Pharaoh's dream in the Old Testament of the Bible. Joseph correctly interpreted the reverie of seven fat and seven lean cows as a forecast of abundance followed by famine.

✦ MANIFESTING ✦

The idea of manifesting your desires has become hugely popular thanks to famous figures such as Oprah Winfrey, yet magicians have understood its power all along. Manifesting is the practice of bringing your desires into reality by intentionally directing your thoughts and energy towards that thing. Its key principle is the law of attraction, meaning that like attracts like, and positive thinking attracts a positive reality.

How to manifest
- Define a clear outcome, but remain open as to how the results might show up.
- Take proactive steps towards your intention. If you're visualizing a new career, start researching it.
- Work with the cycles of the moon for optimum manifesting (see page 37).
- Use magickal rituals to add potency to your manifestations, such as dedicating an altar to your intention, or using candles or herbs to amplify your intentions.
- Now set your manifestation free, and trust that it's working its magick. Obsessing can obstruct its way!
- Remember to say thank you every time a new step towards your goal works out.

✦.✳ ASTROLOGY ✳•✦

We all have a peek at our daily horoscopes from time to time but astrology is a type of divination based on the influence of the stars and planets, and readings depend on their positioning at certain times. The position of the planets at the time of your birth is believed to influence the path your life journey will take, and many people get their birth charts read by a professional astrologer to help them navigate life's ups and downs.

The most famous grimoire of astrological magick is the *Picatrix*, written in Arabic around the eleventh century CE, and republished today, allowing "astro-magick" or planetary magick to enjoy something of a rebirth.

Astro-magick gives you the chance to become an active participant in your fate, rather than feeling that your life is at the whim of the planets. You can work with the special attributes of the planets in your own magickal practice, according to each planet's special day of the week and even its planetary hours.

✦ THE PLANETS ✦

Each planet has its own energy. Check out the specialities of some of the planets below:

Sun: confidence and visibility
Magickal number: 6
Colours: yellow, gold
Offerings: yellow candles, honey, sunflowers

Moon: emotional well-being and fears of scarcity
Magickal number: 9
Colours: white, silver, grey
Offerings: white candles, water, seashells

Saturn: responsibility and resilience
Magickal number: 3
Colours: black, grey
Offerings: dark-coloured candles, other dark or black items, including black coffee and tobacco!

Jupiter: wisdom and abundance
Magickal number: 4
Colours: purple, indigo, yellow, white
Offerings: the more extravagant, the better! Champagne, exotic fruits and oils, frankincense, money

Mars: competitiveness and being assertive
Magickal number: 5
Colours: red
Offerings: red wine, dragon's blood incense or red gemstones, such as carnelian

Venus: love and relationships
Magickal number: 7
Colours: pastels, emerald green
Offerings: fresh flowers, perfume, jewellery

Mercury: communication, travel and technology
Magickal number: 8
Colours: orange, multi-colours
Offerings: items to do with communication and travel, such as letters or keys

Working with planetary days
As well as working with the planets themselves, enhance potency by carrying out your magickal rituals on a certain day:

- **Monday** – Moon
- **Tuesday** – Mars
- **Wednesday** – Mercury
- **Thursday** – Jupiter
- **Friday** – Venus
- **Saturday** – Saturn
- **Sunday** – Sun

✦.✴ NUMEROLOGY ✴•✦

The Greek mathematician and philosopher Pythagoras believed that numbers had their own energies and meanings, and, consequently, numerology is the use of numbers for divination. It's often used in combination with other divinatory tools to bring extra information to a reading.

Although interpretations vary between practitioners, below are the key meanings associated with the numbers 1–9. Once you hit double figures or larger, you add the digits of the number together to get a single digit number (unless your number is a master number), e.g. 13 is represented as $1 + 3 = 4$.

0 – nothingness, void, infinity, before creation
1 – new beginnings, leadership, opportunity
2 – partnerships, harmony/balance and collaboration, sensitivity
3 – creativity, communication
4 – stability, practicality
5 – action, adventure, adaptability
6 – unconditional love, healing, nurturance, hope, compassion
7 – the mind, thought, intellect, wisdom, intuition, gathering information and knowledge
8 – balance, success, achievement
9 – completion, transformation, surrender

✦ MASTER NUMBERS ✦

The master numbers 11, 22 and 33 have special resonance and are considered the most powerful numbers in numerology. They represent the following:

11 - growth, intuition, sensitivity, divine support and guidance

22 - carries the most powerful building and manifesting energy of all numbers

33 - caring, nurturing, creative, healers and guides, high spiritual evolution

Numerology in magickal practice

- Numerology is easy to include in your magickal practice. You could meditate on the energies of your chosen number or include its energy vibration in a spell.

- You can also discover valuable insights about yourself if you add up your birth date to reveal your life path number. For example, 17 October 1992 = 1 + 7 + 1 + 0 + 1 + 9 + 9 + 2 = 30, which is represented as 3 + 0 = 3, meaning your life path number is 3.

- There are many different types of calculations that you can do to uncover things such as your name number or your personality type.

- Knowing the numerology that applies to your own life can help you to see goals more clearly and reach your full potential.

✦.✷ THE *I CHING* ✷•✦

One of the oldest books in existence, the *I Ching*, is an ancient Chinese divination text from around 1000 BCE. An oracle that can be used to help with decision-making, it can help us to successfully navigate life's trickier moments.

Said to have been written by Fu Xi, it's known as the *Book of Changes* in English and inspired the mystical belief systems of Taoism and Confucianism. The psychoanalyst Carl Jung even worked with the *I Ching* both personally and in consultations with his patients.

The *I Ching* recognizes that people inherently have both positive and negative traits, and teaches positive qualities, such as peace, restraint and adaptability, while advising against negative actions of the ego, such as greed, arrogance and anger.

This magickal method works via cleromancy, a divination carried out by choosing lots. Cleromancy can take various forms, such as picking a card or a straw. While it can be argued that the outcome depends on chance, some believe that it is the work of magickal forces, revealing the will of God or spirit.

The *I Ching* manual will guide you in how to interpret your reading, based on 8 symbolic trigrams and 64 hexagrams, which are interpreted in line with the principles of yin and yang. Yarrow stalks were used to cast lots in traditional practice, as they were considered to come from a sacred plant. Modern versions of the book suggest shaking three coins in your hand and dropping them.

You'll be advised on anything from the best course of action to knowing when to take a step back, reflect and head to a space of meditation and stillness. Whatever you need to do in your current situation, the *I Ching* will advise you!

One of the wonderful things about this method of divination is that anyone can consult the *I Ching* and be able to communicate directly with spirit. No training is required, as the act of divination is magick itself.

Taking your future into your own hands and being part of your own and collective universal change is what magick is all about!

✦ PSYCHOMETRY ✦

Have you ever seen TV psychics receiving information just by holding somebody's ring or watch? Also known as token-object reading, this is the skill of psychometry, and it's a great place for beginners to start learning to read psychic energy.

Translated from the Greek, psychometry means "measuring the soul", and the practice was given its name by American physician Joseph Rodes Buchanan in 1842. He believed that we leave energetic residue on the objects we touch, stemming from our feelings, thoughts and actions. Those sensitive to energy can read "the soul" from the energetic vibrations left on an object. Psychometry can be carried out with any object belonging to another.

How to read an object

1. Hold the object in your hand. The more contact the owner has had with it, the more energy it'll hold.

2. Close your eyes and take a deep breath.

3. Mentally ask about the object. For example, who owns it? What experiences, thoughts or feelings did they have while they possessed it?

4. Allow any images, emotions or memories to come through.

FULL MOON PROSPERITY SPELL

Try this Wiccan spell to improve your finances, enhanced by the power of the full moon.

You will need:
- Cauldron (or pot or bowl)
- Water
- Silver coin

Method

1. On a night when the full moon is bright, fill your cauldron with drinking water.

2. Drop your coin in the water, and place the cauldron where the moon will be able to shine on it, such as a windowsill or a table by the window.

3. Create your own chant, drawing on the power of the full moon to enhance the flow of abundance in your life.

4. Leave the water out in the moonlight all night.

5. Take the coin out of the cauldron the following morning, and empty the water onto your garden, or into a flowerpot.

6. Carry the coin with you for a week, then spend it, launching its wealth energy into the universe.

CASTING A WHITE MAGICK LOVE SPELL

A primary principle of white magick is that it should not undermine the will of another. Casting a love spell on a particular person to attract them towards you would be considered black magick – trying to control the will of another. A white magick love spell would involve setting out your desired qualities in a partner, leaving it up to supernatural wisdom to find that perfect person.

Here's a spell for attracting a partner – with the best of intentions!

You will need:
- Altar
- Chosen items such as herbs and figurines
- Paper and pen (optional)

Method
1. Have your intention clear. Know exactly what you want and remember: positive thoughts only! Consider what's important to you in a relationship.

2. Set up your altar and select items to enhance a love spell. You could choose from appropriate herbs, such as cinnamon, jasmine or basil, or a figurine of a deity, such as Selene, Aphrodite or Freyja, all goddesses of love.

3. Think about the qualities you want in a partner, and place objects on your altar that represent those things. How about a fiery chilli for passion? Or a picture of an owl if you'd like to attract someone wise or intelligent? Feel free to get creative!

4. Cast a circle (see page 96). Make sure your altar (and you!) are inside the circle. Face towards your altar.

5. Meditate on your intention and focus on the objects you've selected. You could pray to deities or even use a wand to point at the objects and channel your energy and intention towards them.

6. If you wish, recite any incantations or perform any rituals you deem appropriate for your spell. You could create your own spell or use some established ones that you've researched beforehand. Remember not to use any negative words or actions.

HOME PROTECTION SPELL

This easy ritual uses the earth element of salt to cleanse and protect your home from negative energies. Salt has always been linked to purity in religious rituals, and in moderate amounts it is essential for helping our body to function properly. In ancient times, it was used in food preservation, wound healing, absorbing negative energies and to scare away bad luck. Perform this ritual as often as you like!

You will need:
- Broom
- Coarse salt, such as rock, sea or Epsom salt

Method
1. Sweep the floor to ensure the space is physically clean. You could use a regular broom, besom or other magickal broom.

2. Place a handful of salt on the floor.

3. Use the broom to sweep the salt over the room. Chant your intentions as you sweep.

4. When you feel that you've cleansed away any lingering negative energies, sweep up the salt and throw it down the toilet. Ask the water to flush away all negativity.

A SPELL FOR RESOLVING PROBLEMS

This Wiccan spell works with the four elements to help you move forwards in a situation where you're feeling stuck.

You will need:

- Bowl of water
- Incense stick
- Crystal of your choice
- White candle
- Matches

Method

1. Arrange everything on an altar, with water facing west, air (incense) facing east, earth (crystal) facing north and fire (candle) facing south.

2. Light the incense, activating the air element.

3. Warm your hands, then hold your crystal. Feel its energy invoke the earth element.

4. Light the candle to invoke fire.

5. Dip your finger into the water to activate water.

6. Invent your own chant that vocalizes your feelings. Visualize an empty road and see yourself moving along it.

7. Allow the candle to burn down completely. Discard the remains and say thank you.

✦ CONCLUSION ✦

Hopefully this book has inspired you to find out more about the mysterious supernatural force that is magick while providing you with some first steps into the craft, from which tools and symbols to work with, to different types of magick.

There are so many magickal groups, beliefs and practices that it's not been possible to cover them all because one of the beauties of magick is its bespoke ability to suit every individual. Although based on ancient ideas and traditions, the evolving history of magick shows the adaptability of the practice while retaining its ancient roots, from deity worship to an affinity with nature.

You can be guided by others in your magickal practice, but ultimately, being a magician will become a practice personal to you as you build the confidence to develop your own incantations and rituals. Whether you choose to practise alone or join another like-minded group for support and guidance, remember that with self-empowerment comes responsibility.

But the mystery of magick is eternal, and the secrets are yours to discover!

✦ FURTHER READING ✦

Books

Allaun, Chris *Upperworld: Shamanism and Magick of the Celestial Realms* (2019, Mandrake of Oxford (UK))

Buckland, Raymond *Wicca for One: The Path of Solitary Witchcraft* (2018, Kensington)

Chapman, Alan *Advanced Magick for Beginners* (2008, Aeon Books)

Guiley, Rosemary Ellen *The Encyclopedia of Witches, Witchcraft and Wicca* (2008, Facts on File)

Murphy-Hiscock, Arin *The Green Witch: Your Complete Guide to the Natural Magic of Herbs, Flowers, Essential Oils, and More (Green Witch Witchcraft Series)* (2017, Adams Media)

Valentine, Robyn *Magickal Tarot: Spreads, Spellwork, and Ritual for Creating Your Life* (2021, Fair Winds Press)

Podcasts

The Queer Witch with Morgan La Feuille
The Witch Wave with Pam Grossman
(Both available on Apple Podcasts)

Website

The Spells8 Forum – https://forum.spells8.com/

HERBAL MAGIC
Lydia Levine

Hardback · ISBN: 978-1-83799-129-7

Step into the enchanting world of herbal recipes, remedies and rituals with this spellbinding guide to the magical power of plants

Including a variety of crafts, spells and rituals, this treasury of herb profiles is the perfect introduction to conjuring your inner power and enriching your life with a little herbal magic. Whether you are drawn to blends and brews or elixirs and potions, the unique natural powers of these bewitching ingredients are ready and waiting for you.

THE LITTLE BOOK OF WITCHCRAFT
Judith Hurrell

Paperback · ISBN: 978-1-80007-407-1

**Discover the wonders of Wicca and learn
how to harness your inner power with this
beginner's guide to white witchcraft**

This book is the perfect introduction to magick and
white witchcraft. Whether you're a budding witch
or simply want to learn more about the world of
spells and sorcery, you'll find everything you need to
understand and start practising this remarkable craft.

Have you enjoyed this book?
If so, find us on Facebook at **Summersdale Publishers**,
on Twitter/X at **@Summersdale** and on Instagram and
TikTok at **@summersdalebooks** and get in touch.
We'd love to hear from you!

www.summersdale.com

IMAGE CREDITS

Cover and throughout – sun and moon © Tanya Antusenok/Shutterstock.
com; leaves, sparkles and moons © lyubava.21/Shutterstock.com; p.4 –
crystal ball © Pixejoo/Shutterstock.com; p.9 – magickal woman © Victoria
Bat/Shutterstock.com; p.17 – cauldron © Azuzl/Shutterstock.com; p.28 –
triquetra © Serhii Borodin/Shutterstock.com, crossed spears © pavlematic/
Shutterstock.com; p.29 – Eye of Horus © Roberto Marantan/Shutterstock.
com, Hamsa © Trimaker/Shutterstock.com; p.30 – pentacle © nu Kristle/
Shutterstock.com, seal of Solomon © bsd studio/Shutterstock.com; p.31
– Mars © Aylin Art Studio/Shutterstock.com, solar cross © Luis Line/
Shutterstock.com; p.32 – Horned God © Zvereva Yana/Shutterstock.
com, Triple Goddess © paw/Shutterstock.com; p.34 – element symbols ©
luma_art/Shutterstock.com; p.35 – element symbols © NeslihanGorucu/
Shutterstock.com; p.42 – the Wheel of the Year © paw/Shutterstock.com